INTRODUCTION

Ask anyone who knows anything about ships which is the most elegant of all vessels in service across the North Sea and they will unhesitatingly reply the **Winston Churchill**.

The fact that the ship remains in service in the 1990's is ample testimony to the skill of her Italian builders and also to the way in which her owners have cared for and maintained her during her illustrious career.

The Company newspaper, the "DFDS Express" used the headline 'A Great Ship takes to the Sea' to mark her entry into service and back in 1967 she was indeed a 'great ship'. Few ferries operating from British ports reached anywhere near her gross tonnage but her size was not her only claim to greatness. The **Winston Churchill** was hailed as a luxury floating hotel, her two class accommodation for just 462 passengers being fitted-out to the highest quality of workmanship and design. A drive-through ship, she allowed roll on-roll off traffic to be carried on the Harwich-Esbjerg route for the first time and with her running partner, the **England**, she was able to ship about 2000 cars a week on the premier route to Denmark.

Such statistics almost pale into insignificance besides the vast capacity of the route's modern flagship, the **Dana Anglia**, but it should be stated that what fitted the requirements of the Company and of the travelling public in 1967, does not necessarily meet the changed needs of the 1990's. Demand has far outgrown her capacity. Although a much-loved vessel, the

Winston Churchill' [...] ighly commercialised wo [...] s are certainly number [...] e for sentimentality – fer [...] more competition than e [...] ere is little doubt that the 'Churchill is a [...] in the eyes of those who sail in her on their summer holidays from North Shields to Esbjerg and of those Faroe Islanders who rely on her as their lifeline with the outside world.

When the time eventually comes for DFDS to retire the North Sea's most beautiful ship, there will be many loyal devotees who will mourn her passing from the stage upon which she has so majestically served for over twenty, rapidly changing, years. Hopefully this publication will serve as a souvenir of her life and times when ships looked like ships and traditional ferry design put aesthetic considerations before commercial necessity. Sad as this may be to the traditionalists, the authors are fully aware that in order to be successful in the nineties, the expectations of both passengers and freight hauliers must be met and surpassed whilst ensuring that the whole operation incorporates all the latest and up-to-date safety requirements and improvements.

Miles Cowsill
Kilgetty, Dyfed.

FERRY Publications

John Hendy
Staplehurst, Kent.

April 1991
ISBN 1 871947 08 1

FOREWORD

I welcome the opportunity of providing a Foreword to this book on the **Winston Churchill** – not least because this popular vessel marked a significant state in the development of North Sea passenger traffic.

Although the **England**, built in 1964, was the pioneer DFDS passenger vessel with drive-on/drive-off facilities to be used between the UK and Scandinavia, access to the car deck was by side ports which limited vehicles to cars and caravans. The **Winston Churchill**, introduced three years later, marked an important step forward in having bow and stern doors which allowed commercial vehicles and trailers to be carried in addition to cars.

The **Winston Churchill** was also the last of our North Sea passenger ships to be built with two class accommodation, being converted to a one class configuration in 1970.

Of course one must not overlook this particular vessel's illustrious name, and the directors of DFDS took the decision to call the new building **Winston Churchill** on hearing of the death of the British statesman and wartime leader.

After obtaining permission for the ship to carry the name from Baroness Churchill, she was invited to perform the naming ceremony – an invitation she graciously accepted.

The naming was held after completion and the new flagship was brought to London especially for this purpose prior to entering service. The ceremony took place on board on 30 May 1967 with the **Winston Churchill** moored off Greenwich –

The **Winston Churchill** *approaching Parkeston Quay for the first time on 29 May 1967. (Robert Spark collection)*

itself a place with strong maritime associations. For all those who were on board it was a memorably and moving occasion.

The name was also a popular choice with the Danish public who recalled **Winston Churchill's** stirring radio broadcasts when the country was occupied during the dark days of war.

After a number of highly successful years on the Harwich-Esbjerg route sailing alongside the **England** and later **Dana Regina**, the **Winston Churchill** was transferred to the Newcastle-Esjberg service in 1978. This was followed by use on seasonal sailings from Newcastle to Gothenburg and from Esbjerg to the Faroe Islands.

In 1987, the **Winston Churchill** began her new career as a cruise ship. She sailed on a series of spring and autumn cruises along the Norwegian coast to the North Cape. In 1989 the cruise programme was extended to include some Baltic itineraries. These attracted a loyal following and for the 1989 series a major refurbishment was carried out to provide even better facilities on board.

Thus the **Winston Churchill** began what might be described as a new lease of life, although she continued in its traditional role as a passenger/car ferry in the summer months.

Passengers appreciated the ship's elegant lines, the use of traditional materials for the interior furnishings and the fact that her size provided an intimate atmosphere.

Because she had become the oldest passenger ship in the Scandinavian Seaways fleet did not mean that she was neglected. Far from it, and in this respect the officers and crew are particularly proud of the **Winston Churchill** and realise

that she enjoys a strong following among ship lovers everywhere. Not surprisingly the ship has been referred to as "something of a treasure within the Danish fleet".

The ship has sailed many thousands of miles, in all weathers, performed remarkably well and been seen in many ports in Britain, Scandinavia and within the Baltic. I hope she will be able to fulfil her present role for some years to come. In the same way I believe that

E.K. Pedersen – Managing Director, DFDS UK Ltd.

this book will provide an informative and interesting souvenir of a friendly and popular vessel.

Ebbe Pedersen
Managing Director, DFDS UK Limited.

The **Winston Churchill** *makes a dramatic scene in this picture, as she is launched into the Mediterranean waters on 25 April 1967. (DFDS)*

POST WAR GROWTH

In 1946, DFDS introduced the splendid motorship **Kronprins Frederik** on their Harwich – Esbjerg link. Three years later she was joined by her sistership **Kronprinsesse Ingrid** and together the twins set the trend for speed and comfort across the North Sea all during the 1950's. Six sailings a week during the peak summer periods were reduced to just two in winter. The ships quickly gained a loyal following but all motor cars had to be loaded by crane into an enclosed hold space – a slow procedure which frequently delayed sailing times and exhausted the limited hold capacity available to them. By the early 1960's the twin vessels were unable to cope with the increased car trade and so the Company went to the Elsinore Shipyard for a new ship which was to be larger and faster and which would incorporate all the latest technical developments and travel trends. The result was the car ferry **England**, which entered service in May 1964. With capacity for as many as 100 cars, the new ship was revolutionary and her presence created greater demand than ever before.

With the **Kronprins Frederik** now switched to the Newcastle (North Shield) routes, the **Kronprinsesse Ingrid** was no suitable running partner for the new car ferry and so it came as little surprise when a second such ship was ordered.

The **England** *berthed at Harwich in January 1966. The side-loading door can be clearly seen in this picture.(John Hendy)*

ENTER THE 'CHURCHILL'

The contract for the building of the new vessel was signed in 1965, the work being awarded to the Italian yard of Cantieri Navali del Tirreno e Riuniti at Riva Trigoso, near Genoa.

Although a similar ship in many ways to the **England**, the new ship was constructed as a drive-through ferry and incorporated bow and stern doors. Sufficient headroom down her centre line also allowed lorries and tourist coaches to be shipped whereas the **England's** side loading car deck prohibited this. High operating speeds of 21 knots allowed he Harwich – Esbjerg crossing to be reduced to 18 hours and this, coupled with rail improvements in England and in Denmark, allowed the London to Copenhagen through service to be greatly improved with overall savings of two hours.

Work in' Italy continued briskly, the vessel being in a high state of completion when she was launched from the beach on 25 April 1967. Evidence of her readiness for service was seen when the ship arrived at Harwich for the first time on 29 May. A large crowd had gathered to see her gracefully sail up the River Stour before berthing at Parkeston Quay. Sirens, from the other ships gathered there, welcomed the new-comer while she, in turn, saluted her thanks. That evening a reception was held on board before just after midnight, she left Harwich for the Thames, reaching her destination just up river from the **Cutty Sark** and the Royal Naval College in the early hours. There on 30 May, she was ready for naming.

In an imaginative and wonderfully apt move, the DFDS

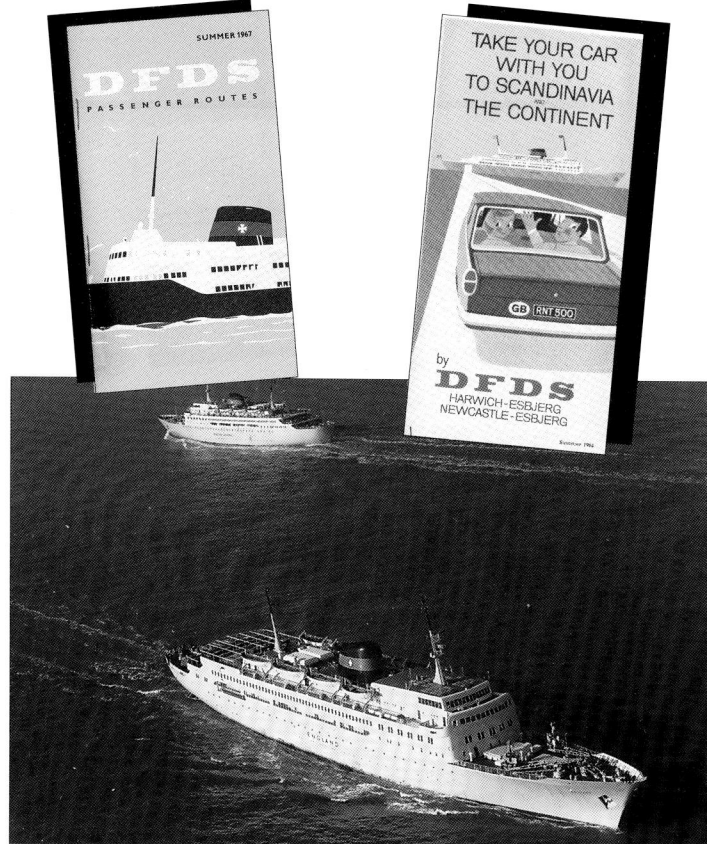

*Sixties partners pass each other in the North Sea. The **England** (pictured right) is inward bound for Harwich, while the **Winston Churchill** is on passage to Denmark.(Foto Flite W 69/664)*

*The **Winston Churchill** in the English Channel en-route from her Italian builders. The 'Churchill' was initially built with four lifeboats on the port and starboard, this was later increased to five a side when her passenger capacity was increased. (Robert Spark collection)*

Board in Copenhagen had written to Lady Churchill asking her permission to name their new luxury passenger vessel after her late husband. Not only did she agree to this request but gladly accepted the invitation to officially name the ship.

Lady Churchill was taken from Greenwich Pier to the ferry at about 11.45 in the Port of London Authority's launch, **Nore**. Although it was pouring with rain at the time, Lady Churchill's beaming smile and easy manner made it a memorable day for all on board. Mr J. Fog-Petersen (Joint Managing Director) assisted Lady Churchill and 62 year old Captain H.M. Thomsen gave her a guided tour of the vessel before she named the ship and unveiled the plaque which reads:

MS WINSTON CHURCHILL
Named on the River Thames
by the Baroness
Spencer-Churchill of Chartwell GBE
on May 30, 1967.

The Company were only too happy to explain to the media just why they had chosen the name of Britain's most famous post-War Prime Minister with which to name their new ship. Consul Warrer, Chairman of DFDS, said that it was a purely emotional decision and that the commercial aspect was never considered. 'Our wish to name this ship **Winston Churchill** stems from a deep sense of grateful veneration for a man who

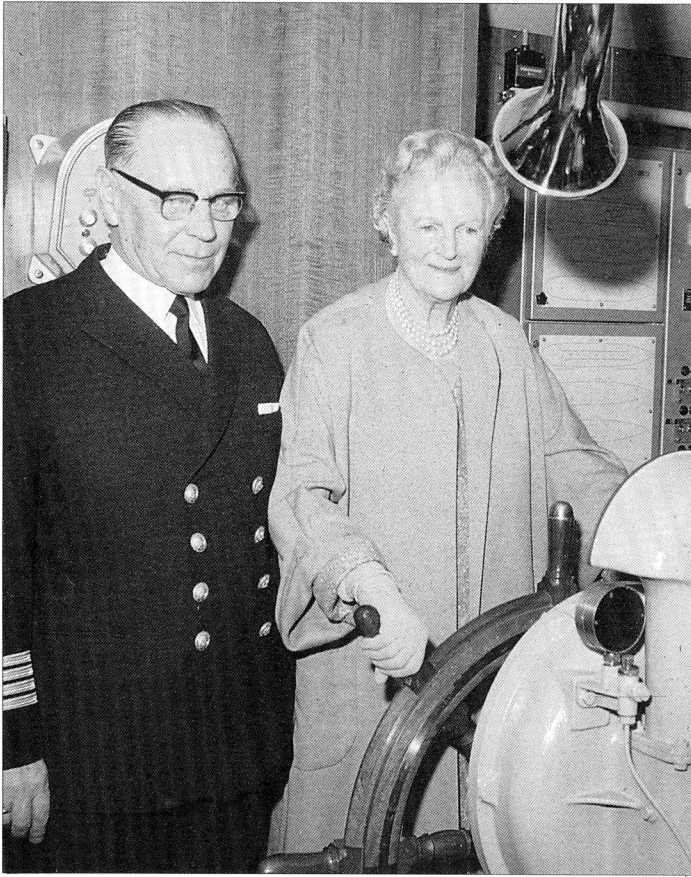

Lady Churchill and Captain Thomsen on the bridge at Greenwich (DFDS collection)

Another view of the **Winston Churchill** *at Greenwich. (Ambrose Greenway)*

gave himself to his country and to the whole free world.' The Danish Ambassador echoed these sentiments when he stated, 'No Dane will ever forget what we owe Winston Churchill as leader of the British people during the last war. He was a shining light in our darkest years.'

After the speeches, Lady Churchill was presented with a silver casket bearing the yard's coat of arms while DFDS presented her with a silver tray inscribed with an outline of the ship.

The maiden voyage of the Company's new flagship duly commenced on 2 June when the ship left Parkeston Quay from newly completed West Portal at 18.00 hrs, arriving at Esbjerg at 12.00 hrs on the following day. The single fare for a car of under 14 ft. in length was just £6.6s (£6.30) while longer cars

The **Winston Churchill** *off Greenwich on 30 May 1967, ready to be named by Lady Churchill. (Robert Spark collection)*

The bust of Sir Winston Churchill in the Dining Room of the vessel.(Miles Cowsill)

A LOOK AROUND

When built, the **Winston Churchill** boasted accommodation for just 462 passengers – 124 in the First Class, 274 in the Second Class and 64 in group accommodation. The ship's luxurious interior represented the best in Danish design, plenty of glazed bulkheads helping to give a largely open-plan appearance in the public rooms.

The First Class lounge was panelled in rosewood and occupied the forward position on the Saloon Deck. The bar was on the port side while the lounge and writing room were situated on the starboard side. Astern of this area was the First Class hall from which one was able to step into the restaurant. Glass walls were used in abundance and, when combined with full-length curtains and more rosewood panelling, helped to create the air of spaciousness. A traditional picture tapestry ,designed by Urup Jensen, was the focal point of the Dining Saloon which could seat 135 passengers. The specially commissioned bust of Sir Winston, much admired by Lady Churchill, occupied pride of place in this most attractive area.

At the after end of the Saloon Deck was the Second Class lounge which was panelled in teak, upholstered in beige and brown and featured a completely glazed after bulkhead. Forward of this, the Second Class restaurant, capable of seating up to 220 passengers, was carefully designed in order to create the feeling of space. This was achieved by splitting-up the centre area from two side "wings" which could be screened-off with sliding doors and full-length curtains so that they could be

were charged £7.18s (£7.80). Second class single fare started as low as £6.10s (£6.50), although the 'basic' fare was £10.3s (£10.15). 'Basic' first class travel was priced at £13.11s (£13.55).

A total of 180 cars or 40 x 20 ft. trailers or a mix of both could be carried on the **Winston Churchill**'s car deck. In addition to this, two cargo holds forward carried 55,656 cu. ft., partly refrigerated. In 1973, this cargo space was reduced when the ship's passenger certificate was increased to 757.

Other statistics which came to light in the early years were that the ship used about 33 tons of oil per crossing, her electric wiring totalled 350 km (217 miles), 45 tons of paint were required to paint her and that annually she sailed a distance equal to going around the world four times!

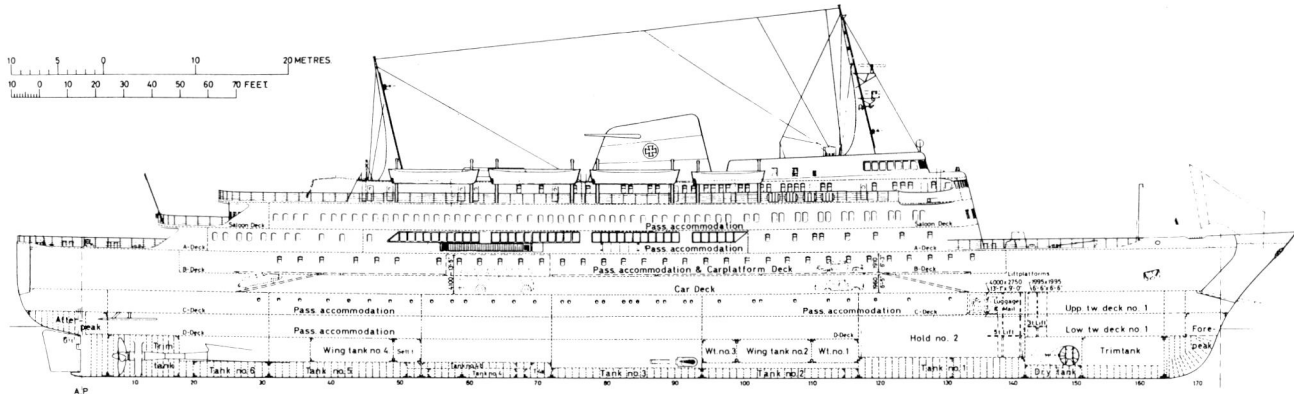

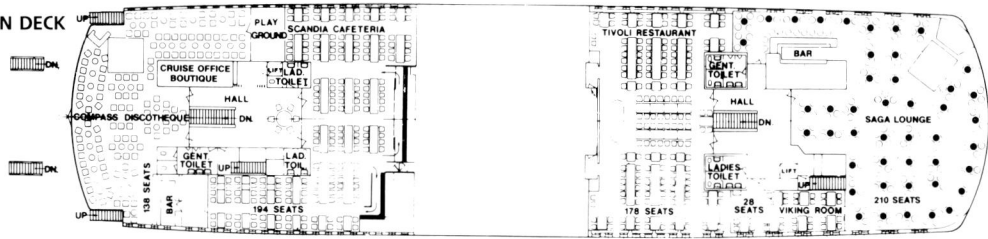

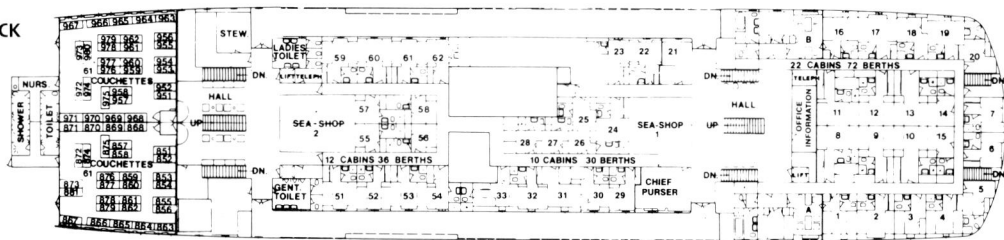

Passengers enjoy the sun on board the **Winston Churchill** *en-route to Harwich in the 'sixties. (DFDS)*

Information Area.

The Scandia Cafeteria.

Saga Lounge.

Tivoli Restaurant.

(All photographs by Miles Cowsill)

used by groups. Teak panelling and an abstract photographic mural helped to create the room's atmosphere. Both Dining Rooms were finished in turquoise/green with light and elegant furniture throughout. The ship's galley was positioned between both restaurants thereby saving the need to 'double-up' on this most important aspect of her operation.

One of the most popular areas on board was the Night Club and Entertainment Centre which was situated at the after end of A Deck. A glazed after bulkhead, behind the bar, afforded splendid views astern while the dance floor was covered in copper and steel. More teak panelling with fabric colours in red and orange helped to create a happy, bright feeling although lighting could be regulated to create the desired atmosphere. The positioning of the Night Club was an important design feature of the **Winston Churchill**. It was placed in this position in order to cause minimum disturbance to those passengers who either wished to rest or to wile away their time in quieter pursuits.

Above the ship's bridge, the Sun Lounge was originally for sole use of the First Class. It offers a wonderful all-round view of the sea and from it, the ship's officers can be seen docking the vessel – always a fascinating experience.

The **Winston Churchill** was one of the first ferries to be equipped with a children's playroom – now a standard fitting in all such ships. The Company recognised that parents too have every right to relax and enjoy themselves while their young ones play in safety.

First Class cabins (one or two berth) were fitted with their

Galley area situated between the restaurant and cafeteria. (Miles Cowsill)

Observation Lounge. (Miles Cowsill)

own washbasins, toilets and showers while those in the Second Class (two or four berth) also contained their own washing facilities. All cabins were air-conditioned, furniture being functional and practical. Two luxury deluxe suites were fitted with their own sitting rooms, bedrooms and a large bathroom complete with all modern conveniences.

Both First and Second Classes were given an Information and Shopping Centre which included the Purser's Office, for cabin allocation, duty-free shops and ship-to-shore telephone facilities. Everything was done to achieve the ambience of a floating luxury hotel. The ship's interior was designed by Kay Kørbing who had previously been responsible for the work on board the **England**. It was obviously a winning formula.

As will be seen, during 1987/89, the **Winston Churchill** received a complete revamp of her passenger accommodation in order to meet the latest requirements and travel trends as seen in her more modern 'sisters'. With the ship also gaining in popularity as a cruise vessel, passengers would be spending up to eight days in their cabins and would also need to use them during daylight hours. A complete rethink resulted and although the interior of the ship we see today is quite different from that as described above, it is still possible to appreciate the sixties panelling in addition to other original work. Comparison of the plans of both the Saloon Deck and A Deck is advised.

On the Sun Deck of the vessel, looking towards the Compass Discotheque entrance on the Saloon Deck. (Miles Cowsill)

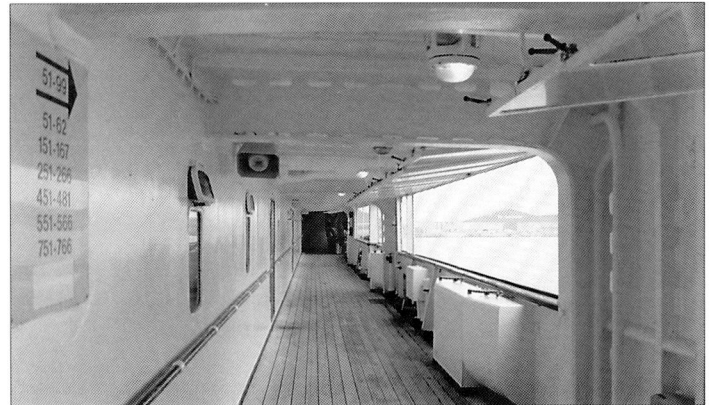

Port side, Promenade Deck looking forward. (Miles Cowsill)

The sheltered Sun Deck area on Boat Deck level. (Miles Cowsill)

Port side, Boat Deck looking forward. (Miles Cowsill)

TECHNICAL

The **Winston Churchill** is powered by two single-acting turbocharged ten-cylinder Italian-built B&W Diesel engines. In tandem they produce some 15,500 i.h.p. at 170 r.p.m.. Each engine transmits 7,750 h.p. through its shaft to a four-bladed propeller. At full speed, the ship can manage 23 knots (42.6 kilometres per hour or 26.1 miles per hour). In addition to the two screws aft, the ship is also fitted with a bow-thrust unit of about 1000 h.p. This is operated from the bridge and allows the ship greater manoeuvrability when in the enclosed confines of harbour. Sperry fin stabilisers help to counter rough weather and are able to exert a combined pressure of 56 tons. When in operation, each fin (measuring about 3.25 square metres) can be turned 20 degrees up or down. The double gyro system registers heeling angles and rolling speeds and automatically regulates the hydraulics which activate the shafts and fins. In calm weather, the fins are retracted into the ship's hull.

The crew of 116 comprised of 76 catering staff, 21 deck staff with 16 in the engine room. Original life-saving equipment gave 572 passenger spaces in the lifeboats in addition to extra capacity in a number of large, self-inflatable, life rafts. The total was far in excess of passenger and crew numbers and considerably more than the statutory amount of life-saving equipment which was required by law. With the current increase in passenger numbers carried, this all-important aspect of the **Winston Churchill**'s equipment has subsequently been increased.

Apart from the **Winston Churchill**'s vehicle decks, the ship was built with a large insulated cargo compartment capable of accommodating up to 33,000 cubic feet. It could be refrigerated to minus 4 degrees celsius thereby preserving the considerable cargoes of dairy and bacon produce which have traditionally been imported into Britain from Denmark. With the increase in roll-on roll-off traffic, the crane-loaded cargo hold was less-used and in 1973, this area was reduced in size at which time extra cabins were fitted thereby raising the ship's passenger capacity.

Looking forward in the early morning light into the depths of the North Sea. (Miles Cowsill)

DFDS

The beautiful way to Scandinavia

Looking aft as the stern door opens off the linkspan at Newcastle. (Miles Cowsill)

Builders' plate.(Miles Cowsill)

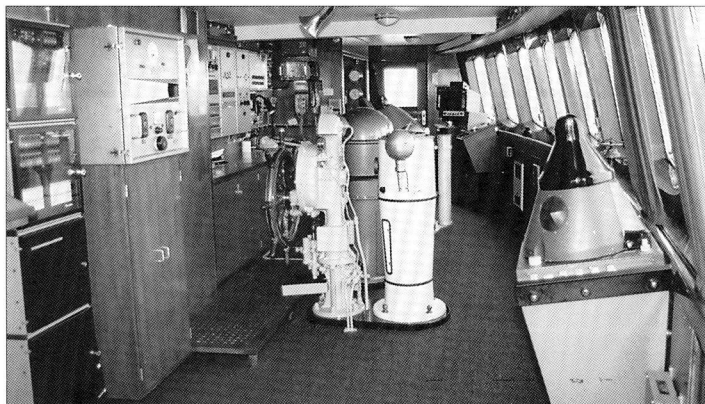

Wheelhouse. (Miles Cowsill)

*The **Winston Churchill** arriving at Esbjerg. (Ken Ling)*

A stern view of the **Winston Churchill** *in the River Stour.(DFDS)*

SUMMER 1969
1st June - 27th September

The
**SCANDINAVIAN
ROUTE**
to
DENMARK - NORWAY - SWEDEN - FINLAND

via **HARWICH—ESBJERG**

D F D S

THE UNITED STEAMSHIP COMPANY LIMITED
COPENHAGEN

**DFDS
SEAWAYS**

1 Oct 1975
30 Apl 1976   **75/76**

TIMETABLE AND FARES

**U.K.—
DENMARK**

**DENMARK—
NORWAY**

Early days for the
Winston Churchill
*showing cars driving
off at Esbjerg.
(Robert Spark
collection)*

*The **Winston Churchill** (left) and **England** laid up at Esbjerg in February 1982. (Ambrose Greenway)*

*The **Winston Churchill** arriving at Harwich in the early 'seventies. (Ambrose Greenway)*

WINSTON CHURCHILL – YEAR BY YEAR

1965 Contract signed for the building of the ship

1967 Ship due to be launched in Italy on 22 April but adverse weather conditions delayed this for three days. Named at Greenwich by Lady Churchill on 30 May. Maiden voyage from Harwich to Esbjerg on 2 June. She becomes Denmark's newest, largest and fastest ferry. Replaces **Kronprinsesse Ingrid** which moves to Newcastle service. Running partner, **England** starts Caribbean cruising during winter months.

1970 During April a new disco and couchette lounge (116 passengers) are fitted. As from start of winter service on 1 October, the ship becomes one class.

1971 The Company changes its legal title to DFDS A/S. The long-established, full title of, 'Det Forenede Dampskibs-Selskab A/S (The United Steamship Company), Copenhagen' is abandoned. Captain H.H.Thomsen, the ship's first Master, retires in December.'

1973 The **Winston Churchill**'s cargo space is converted to additional passenger cabins. Passenger certificate increased to 750.

1974 The **Dana Regina** joins the **Winston Churchill** on the Harwich to Esbjerg route on 8 July. The **England** is switched to the Newcastle service.

1976 DFDS order new ship for Harwich – Esbjerg service as traffic figures soar. Service now becomes daily all year round.

1978 Company adopt trading name of 'DFDS Danish Seaways'. **Dana Anglia** runs maiden voyage on 5 June replacing the **Winston Churchill** which switches to the Tyne services running a single voyage to Esbjerg and two trips to Gothenburg – the latter a joint service with Tor Line.

1979 The **Winston Churchill**'s bleakest hour. The ship runs aground on Vinga Island soon after leaving Gothenburg in a gale on 27 August. Passengers safely evacuated – ship badly damaged. Drydocked at the Swedish port before repairs in Denmark which involve extensive hull repair, removal of engines and port propeller shaft, new screws and complete renewal of the engine room electrics.

1980 Ship returns to service on 25 March. 'Welcome Back' mini-cruises offered.

1981 DFDS acquire Prins Line and then Tor Line. **Dana Gloria** runs her maiden voyage to Newcastle on 3 June. **Winston Churchill** returns to Harwich in May to cover for the **Dana Anglia**.

1982 **Winston Churchill** returns to the Harwich service in May to cover for the **Dana Regina**. **England** withdrawn from service at end of summer season.

The sun strikes across the decks of vessel on the starboard side. (Miles Cowsill)

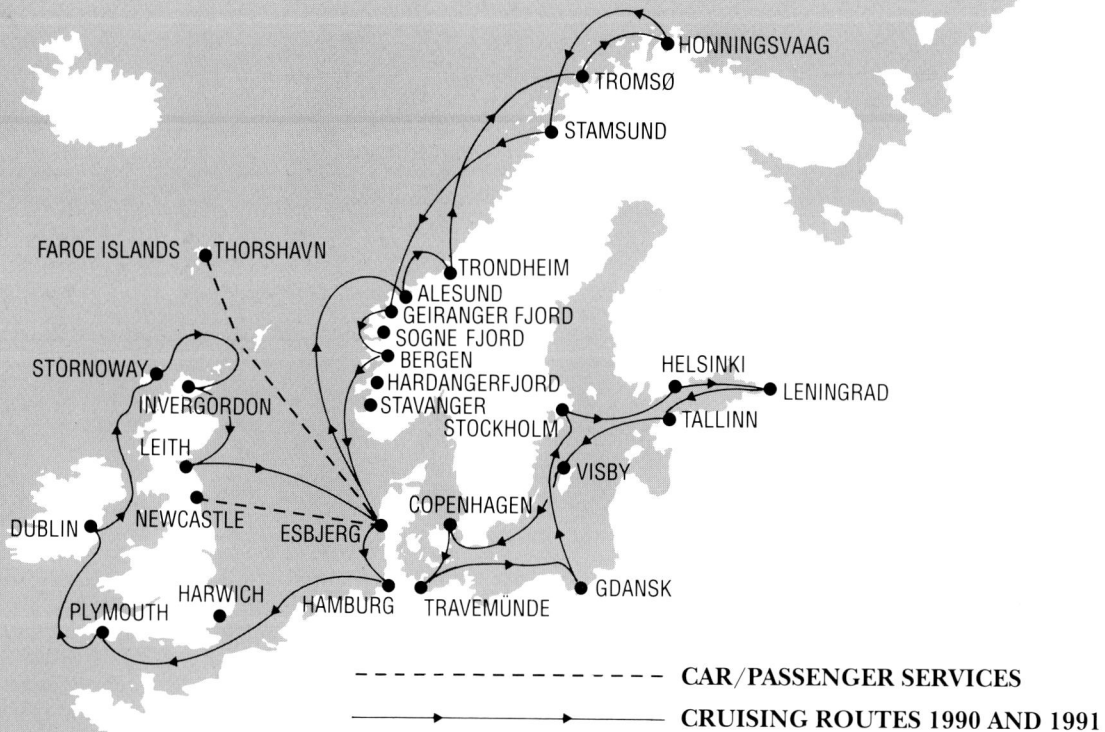

HONNINGSVAAG
TROMSØ
STAMSUND
TRONDHEIM
ALESUND
GEIRANGER FJORD
SOGNE FJORD
BERGEN
HARDANGERFJORD
STAVANGER

FAROE ISLANDS   THORSHAVN

STORNOWAY
INVERGORDON
LEITH

HELSINKI
LENINGRAD
TALLINN
STOCKHOLM
VISBY

DUBLIN   NEWCASTLE
ESBJERG
COPENHAGEN

PLYMOUTH   HARWICH   HAMBURG   TRAVEMÜNDE   GDANSK

- - - - - - - - - - - -   CAR/PASSENGER SERVICES

━━━━━▶━━━━━▶━━━   CRUISING ROUTES 1990 AND 1991

CRUISING AND FERRY OPERATIONS 1990 & 1991

1983 Failure of DFDS cruising in USA results in cut-backs. Tyne – Oslo (operated by the **England** since 1981) is axed and the **Winston Churchill** is one of 7 ships offered for sale. The **England** is sold to Cunard Line for ferry service from Cape Town to the Falklands on charter to Ministry of Defence. All UK operations are marketed under the name of 'DFDS Seaways'.

1984 Seasonal service from June to August includes regular Faroe Islands sailings from Copenhagen.

1985 **Winston Churchill** commences seasonal service in June also running to Torshavn (Faroe Islands) from Esbjerg again. Ship is sold to parent company, J. Lauritzen, for about DanKr 40 million in order to boost DFDS finances.

1986 During August, DFDS buy back the **Winston Churchill** from Lauritzen. Sails to Plymouth, with the **England**, for a naval exercise with the British Ministry of Defence after which she sails to Copenhagen for Kr.2 million refit.

1987 The ship receives a major refit in readiness for a completely new phase in her illustrious career. Before and after her summer season of peak-service ferry runs, the **Winston Churchill** is tried on a series of Norwegian coastal cruises which are a great success and are limited to just 400 people.

1988 Eight more Norwegian coastal cruises operate during May, August and September calling at Aalesund, Trondheim and Tromso on the way to the North Cape (the northern most point in Europe). Calls at

The **Winston Churchill** *at Esbjerg loading for Newcastle on 24 February 1982. (Ambrose Greenway)*

The **Winston Churchill** *on the River Tyne following her return to service after her accident, when she ran aground after leaving Gothenburg. (Robert Spark collection)*

An impressive view of the **Winston Churchill** *showing to the full extent the wealth of outside deck space. (Foto Flite 56015)*

Honningsvaag (near the North Cape), Narvik, Geiranger Fjord and Bergen are made during the return south. Scandinavian Seaways is adopted as the brand name at the end of the year

1989 The ship is sent to the Nobiskrug Yard in Rendsburg (Germany) for a £2 million refurbishment and modifications which includes the gutting of B Deck and the conversion of many cabins to Pullman, day room, use. The former First Class lounge is completely rebuilt and capacity is increased by 50 to 250 seats. By this time, the area is called the Saga Lounge, while the former First Class Dining Room is the Tivoli Restaurant. The old Second Class Restaurant – now a cafeteria – is the Scandia Cafeteria while the Night Club is now the Compass Discotheque. Ship commences summer ferry service from the Tyne on 9 June. Esbjerg services end on 13 August while Gothenburg services operate between 18 June – 27 August. Following this, the ship commences a series of seven day North Cape, Leningrad cruises. A 92% load factor is reported. During the winter of 1989/90, the ship is used as a hotel for refugees in Malmo, Sweden.

1990 Cruises of the Norwegian coast, the Baltic Sea and Around Britain cruise included in 1990 programme Plymouth, Dublin, Stornoway, Invergordon and Leith. Newcastle – Esbjerg and Faroe Islands services from 18 June to 20 August.

The **Winston Churchill** *in an all white livery arriving at Harwich. (DFDS)*

In the Stour estuary off Parkeston Quay. The 'Churchill' is pictured here in her revised all-white colour scheme with a dark blue line along the hull.
(Robert Spark collection)

1991 A new eight day Norwegian Fjords cruise is included in the cruise itinerary calling at Hardangerfjord, Bergen, Sognefjord and Geiranger Fjord. Visits to Trondheim, and Stavanger complete the week. The popular nine day, 2500 mile North Cape cruise continues as does the Leningrad and Baltic Capitals Cruise which starts and ends at the German port of Travemunde. Calls are made at Gdynia, Stockholm, Helsinki, Leningrad, Tallinn and Visby. The 12 cruises operate during May, August, September and October.

Tyne ferry season operates between 13 June and 18 August.

The **Winston Churchill** mirrored in the Geiranger Fjord. (DFDS)

Dressed overall in Dublin during her round Britain cruise in September 1990. (Gordon Hislip)

1. The handsome looking **Winston Churchill** arriving at Esbjerg from Newcastle on 10 August 1991. (Miles Cowsill)

2. A fresh morning scene off the Danish coast, with the **Winston Churchill** on passage to the Faroe Islands.(DFDS)

Tor Scandinavia. *(Foto Flite 79060)*

Tor Britannia. *(Foto Flite 84019)*

OPERATING PARTNERS OF THE 'NINETIES IN THE NORTH SEA

Dana Anglia. *(Foto Flite 85083)*

Hamburg. *(DFDS)*

· · · · · · · · · · WINSTON CHURCHILL · · · · · · · · · ·

GENERAL INFORMATION

Port of Registry .... Esbjerg
Building No./Yard .... 277/C.N.R. Genoa, Italy.
Danish Register No. 10287
Launched .... 25 April 1967
Signal Letters .... OVOD 2
Crew & Officers 115
Trade Limits .... Short international voyages
Passengers 750
Cabins .... 219 cabins/628 berths
Couchettes 122
Cars 180
Speed .... 22 knots

PRINCIPAL DIMENSIONS

Length Overall .... 461'6" (140,67m)
Breadth extreme .... 67'5" (20,55m)
Top of mast over keel .... 132'11"(40,50m)
Draft fully loaded .... 19'5" (5,97m)

TONNAGE

Gross 8658
Nett 4488

MACHINERY

BHP/RPM .... 2 x 7000/170
Propelling Machinery .... 2 CNTR/B&W-1050-VT2BF-110
Auxiliary Machinery .... 4 CNTR/B&W-725-MTBH-40
Fuel consumption per 24 hours .... 53 ts.Heavy Fuel 1500sec. Redw.1
Stabiliser .... Sperry

A busy scene at the port of Esbjerg. The **Winston Churchill** *is pictured in the centre with, behind her the* **Dana Anglia**. *Nearer to the camera is the ro-ro freighter* **Stafford**. *(Robert Spark collection)*

The **Winston Churchill** *at Honningsvaag. This port of call on her Norwegian cruises takes in the North Cape.(Robert Spark)*

ACKNOWLEDGEMENTS

The authors are grateful for the assistance of all those who have kindly contributed to this publication.

Firstly we would like to thank Mr E.K. Pedersen, Managing Director, DFDS UK Ltd, for agreeing to write the Foreword and also for following the project with interest and enthusiasm.

The authors would like to express their gratitude to Robert Spark for all his help with the publication and for providing some outstanding pictures for the project.

Thanks must go the authors' wives, Linda and Stella for all their assistance and support and also to their partner Richard Danielson.

The following are thanked for photographs and information.

Ambrose Greenway, Gordon Hislip, Kay Kington (DFDS), Ken Ling, Bernard McCall and Jane Rees (DFDS).

We would like to thank our good friends at Foto Flite, Philip Neumann, Director, and Nigel Scutt for all their help with photographic material. Most of the outstanding aerial photographs in this book have been kindly provided by Foto Flite; these and many other historical pictures of ships of different shapes and sizes can be purchased from the company. For further details and price list, contact: Foto Flite, Littlestone Road, New Romney, Kent, TN28 8LW, England.(Tel: 0679 64891, Telex: 96303)

Finally we would like to thank Ian Smith, Bézier Design Ltd, Pembroke and Andrew Lowe of Haven Colourprint, Pembroke Dock for all their assistance with design and printing of the book.

Choose a cruise with a difference this year. Scandinavian Seaways are offering a choice of three cruises aboard the m.s. Winston Churchill, taking in the spectacular beauty of Norway's fjords and coast or travelling around the capital cities of the Baltic to Russia.

Whichever you choose, when you travel the Scandinavian Sea Way, you are assured of a unique cruising experience. While the new Norwegian Fjord Cruise takes in the dramatic splendour of the fjords and mountains, the coastal cruise, starting from the lively fishing port of Esbjerg, offers the passenger nine days of breathtaking coastal scenery.

The Baltic Cruise takes in Stockholm, Helsinki, Visby, Tallin, Gdansk and Leningrad, and gives you plenty of time ashore to explore the beauty and architectural splendour of these historic cities.

All three cruises take place aboard the sleek white m.s. Winston Churchill, a memorable experience in itself. The pace is leisurely, the atmosphere informal. First class cuisine, lots of onboard entertainment and a friendly crew ensure a relaxed, enjoyable time. So enjoy the voyage of a lifetime The Scandinavian Sea Way.

Three cruises with one thing in common. They're different.

Please send me my Scandinavian Seaways brochure.

Name

Address

Postcode

Send to Scandinavian Seaways, Marketing Department, Scandinavia House, Parkeston Quay, Harwich, Essex CO12 4QG

THE SCANDINAVIAN SEA WAY

SCANDINAVIAN SEAWAYS